Workbook 2

with Digital Pack

American English

Susan Rivers

Series Editor: Lesley Koustaff

CAMBRIDGE

Shaftesbury Road, Cambridge CB2 8EA, United Kingdom

One Liberty Plaza, 20th Floor, New York, NY 10006, USA

477 Williamstown Road, Port Melbourne, VIC 3207, Australia

314–321, 3rd Floor, Plot 3, Splendor Forum, Jasola District Centre, New Delhi – 110025, India

103 Penang Road, #05–06/07, Visioncrest Commercial, Singapore 238467

Cambridge University Press & Assessment is a department of the University of Cambridge.

We share the University's mission to contribute to society through the pursuit of education, learning and research at the highest international levels of excellence.

www.cambridge.org
Information on this title: www.cambridge.org/9781009798655

© Cambridge University Press & Assessment 2016, 2024

First published 2016
Updated edition 2024

20 19 18 17 16 15 14 13 12 11 10 9 8 7 6 5 4 3

Printed in Poland by Opolgraf

A catalogue record for this publication is available from the British Library

ISBN 978-1-009-79865-5 Workbook with Digital Pack Level 2
ISBN 978-1-009-79858-7 Student's Book with eBook Level 2
ISBN 978-1-009-79866-2 Teacher's Book with Digital Pack Level 2
ISBN 978-1-107-52796-6 Flashcards Level 2

Additional resources for this publication at www.cambridge.org/guesswhatue

Contents

Hello again!

1 Order the letters. Look and draw lines.

1 eLo ___Leo___ **2** dvaiD _____ **3** neB _____

4 iiaOvl _____ **5** aTin _____

2 Look at Activity 1 and put a check ✓.

1	This is Ben.	yes ☐	no ✓
2	This is David.	yes ☐	no ☐
3	This is Leo.	yes ☐	no ☐
4	This is Olivia.	yes ☐	no ☐
5	This is Tina.	yes ☐	no ☐

3 **Listen and stick.**

4 **Look, read, and match.**

①

②

This is my ←	nine.
Her →	friend.
She's	name's Sue.

This is my	eight.
He's	name's Dan.
His	brother.

My picture dictionary → Go to page 84: Check the words you know and trace.

Listen and circle the name.

(Tom) / Don

Pam / Pat

Rick / Nick

Katy / Mary

  Draw and say. Then write and circle.

This is my friend. His name's Alex. He's nine.

This is _____ .
His / Her name's _____ .
He's / She's _____ .

7 **Look, read, and circle the answer.**

1

What's this?

(It's a door.) / They're doors.

2

What are these?

It's a pencil. / They're pencils.

3

What's this?

It's an eraser. / They're erasers.

4

What are these?

They're pens. / It's a pen.

8   **Look and write.**

1

What are ____*these*____ ?

____*They're books*____ .

2

What's _____ ?

It's _____ .

3

What _____ ?

_____ .

4

What _____ ?

_____ .

9 🎧 0.12 **Read and number. Then listen and check.**

a
Wow! What a big surprise!
And look, Ben! Your lion!

b
This is iPal.
Hello, Ben! Let's play.

c
Stand here. You hold iPal.

d
Oh, dear! Help!
Don't worry.

e
This is our tree house.
We have a surprise for you!

1

f
Do you like animals?
Yes, I do.

10 **What's missing? Look and draw. Then stick.**

I play with my friends.

a

b

c

11 **Trace the letters.**

The rabbit can run.
The lion is lazy.

12 **0.15** **Listen and circle *l* or *r*.**

1
l (r)

2
l r

3
l r

4
l r

What kind of **art** is it?

1 Look, read, and circle the word.

1

photograph / (drawing)

2

photograph / painting

3
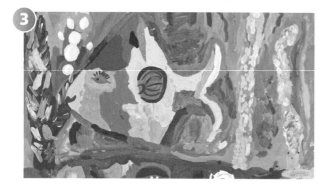
sculpture / painting

4

drawing / sculpture

2 Look and copy the painting.

Evaluation

1 **Look and write the name.**

1	2	3	4	5
L e o	T _ _ _	B _ _	O _ _ _ _ _	D _ _ _ _

2 **What's your favorite part? Use your stickers.**

story   song   video

3 **Puzzle** **What's different? Circle and write.**
Then go to page 93 and write the letters.

____ ____ ____
      17   10

Transportation

1 **Look, read, and check ✓ or put an ✗.**

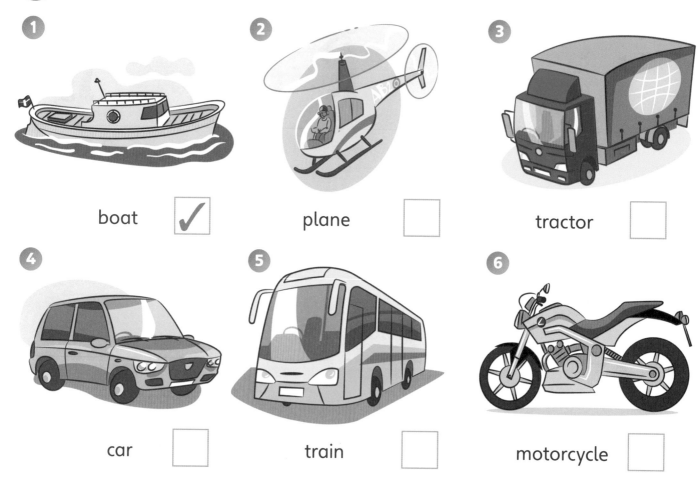

1. boat ✓
2. plane ☐
3. tractor ☐
4. car ☐
5. train ☐
6. motorcycle ☐

2 **Follow the transportation words.**

Start →	train	truck	ruler	chair
	desk	bus	plane	camera
	book	painting	helicopter	table
	pencil	drawing	tractor	boat

Good job!

3 🎧 1.05 📑 Listen and stick.

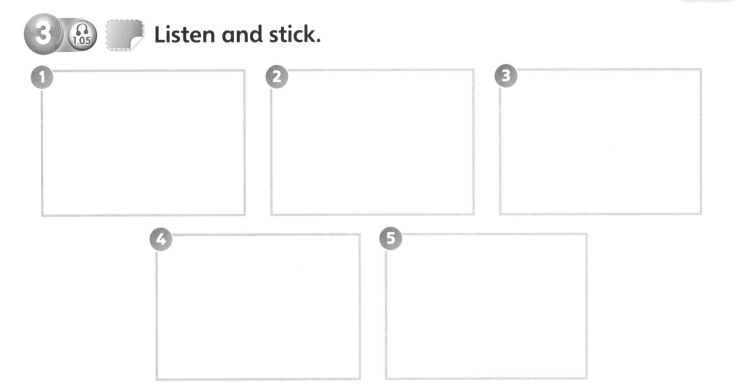

1 | 2 | 3
4 | 5

4 Think Look, read, and write the words.

truck   boat   helicopter   car   motorcycle   plane   train   bus

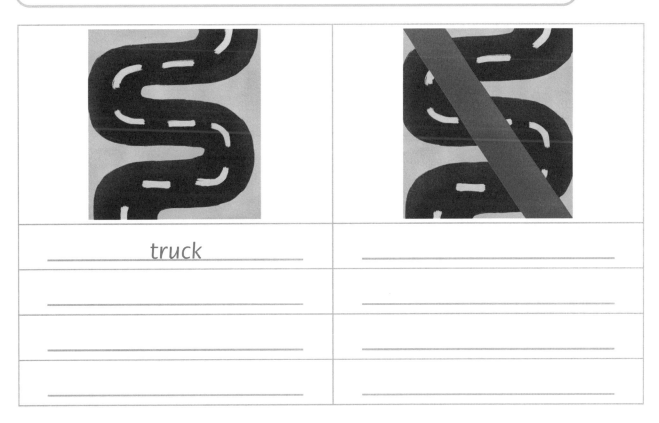

truck

_____

_____

_____

My picture dictionary Go to page 85: Check the words you know and trace.

5 🎧 1.08 Listen and check ✓.

6 Look at the pictures and say.

In picture a, he has a car. In picture b, he has a bus.

7 Look, read, and circle the answer.

1

Does she have a boat?
Yes, she does. / No, she doesn't.

2

Does he have a tractor?
Yes, he does. / No, he doesn't.

3

Does he have a plane?
Yes, he does. / No, he doesn't.

4

Does she have a helicopter?
Yes, she does. / No, she doesn't.

8 Look at the picture and answer the questions.

1 Does he have a train?
   No, he doesn't.

2 Does she have a boat?
   _____

3 Does she have a tractor?
   _____

4 Does he have a bus?
   _____

9 Draw and say. Then circle and write.

This is my friend.
He / She has a
_____ .

10 🎧 1.12 Read and write the letter. Then listen and check.

a Yes, of course. **b** It's OK. **c** Does Ben have a robot?

d Wow! The helicopter is iPal! **e** Thank you. This is fun!

f Ben has a helicopter!

1

f

Let's go to the park!

2

No, he doesn't. It's a helicopter.

3

Can I have a turn, please?

4

Be careful, iPal!

5

Sorry. Now let's play with my helicopter!

6

What's missing? Look and draw. Then stick.

I take turns. ☺

 **Trace the letters.**

A gorilla on the grass. A hippo in the house.

 **Listen and match the pictures with *g* or *h*.**

1 2 3 4

 g  h

Value   Pronunciation: *g, h*   **17**

Where is the transportation?

1 **Look, read, and circle the words.**

1

on land
(on water)
in the air

2

on land
on water
in the air

3

on land
on water
in the air

4

on land
on water
in the air

5

on land
on water
in the air

6

on land
on water
in the air

2 **Look and draw. Say.**

It's a helicopter. It's in the air.

Evaluation

1 (Think) **Look, match, and write the word.**

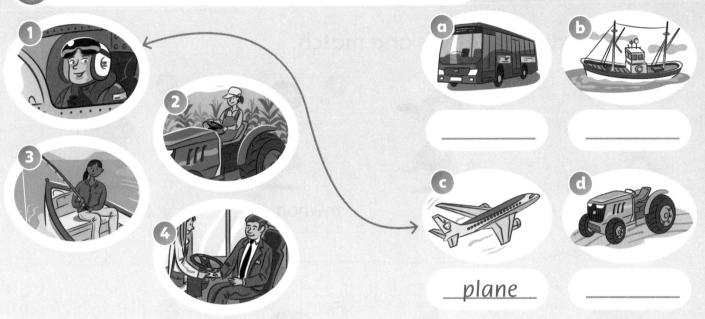

plane

2 **What's your favorite part? Use your stickers.**

story   song   video

3 (Puzzle) **What's different? Circle and write.**
Then go to page 93 and write the letters.

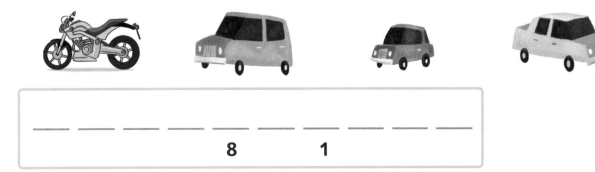

8   1

2 Pets

1 (Think) **Order the letters and match.**

1 nma _man_

2 lirg _____

3 mwnoa _____

4 yob _____

a soeum _____

b hifs _____

c ogd _____

d tac _cat_

2 **What's next? Look and circle the word.**

1 (girl) / boy

2 fish / frog

3 baby / woman

4 cat / dog

3 🎧 2.05 Listen and stick.

1
2
3

4
5

4 Write the words and find.

1

men

2

3

4

```
c  h  i  l  d  r  e  n
n  b  j  k  l  o  p  l
b  c  m  e  n  s  a  o
c  y  m  b  c  g  h  j
v  t  m  w  o  m  e  n
m  e  e  t  y  u  k  a
a  w  b  a  b  i  e  s
q  n  e  r  t  f  n  c
```

My picture dictionary → Go to page 86: Check the words you know and trace.

5 Look, write the words, and match.

ugly   happy   old   beautiful   sad   young

1 _ugly_

a

2 _____

b

3 _____

c

6 Look, read, and check ✓.

1   **2**   **3**   **4**

1 They're happy. ✓   They're sad. ☐

2 It's big. ☐   It's small. ☐

3 She's young. ☐   She's old. ☐

4 He's beautiful. ☐   He's ugly. ☐

7 (About Me) Draw and say. Then write.

This is my cat. It's small. It's beautiful.

This is my _____ . It's _____ . It's _____ .

8 🎧 2.09 Listen and circle the answer.

1

Yes, she is. / No, she isn't.

2

Yes, they are. / No, they aren't.

3

Yes, it is. / No, it isn't.

4

Yes, he is. / No, he isn't.

9 Look at the picture and answer the questions.

1 Is it beautiful? ___No, it isn't.___   **2** Are they happy? _____

3 Is it ugly? _____   **4** Are they old? _____

5 Are they young? _____   **6** Are they sad? _____

cat   ~~frog~~   beautiful   What's   you   sad

1

Look! What's that?

It's a _frog_ !

2

It's Aunt Sue! Hello.

Oh, dear! She's _____.

3

Can we help?

Yes, please. I can't find my _____.

4

Mr. Tom. He's big … and he's _____ !

What's his name?

5

_____ that?

6

Thank _____.

You're welcome!

11 **What's missing? Look and draw. Then stick.**

I am helpful. ☺

a

b

c

12 **Trace the letters.**

A fox with a fish. A vulture with vegetables.

13 (2.14) **Listen and check ✓ v or f.**

1	v ☐	f ✓	2	v ☐	f ☐
3	v ☐	f ☐	4	v ☐	f ☐

What do animals need?

1 Look, read, and match.

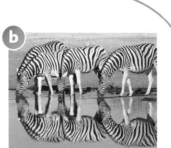

1 Animals need food.

2 Animals need water.

3 Animals need shelter.

4 Animals need sleep.

2 Look at the picture and check ✔ the box.

1 A mouse needs shelter.	☐
2 A mouse needs food.	☐
3 A mouse needs water.	☐

Evaluation

1 **Read and write the answer.**

1 This pet can climb trees. It likes mice and fish.	_cat_
2 This pet swims in water. It doesn't have legs.	_____
3 This pet is very small. It has four short legs and a long tail.	_____
4 This pet likes the water. It has long legs and can jump.	_____
5 This pet has four legs and a tail. It isn't a cat.	_____

2 **What's your favorite part? Use your stickers.**

story   song   video

3 **Puzzle** **What's different? Circle and write. Then go to page 93 and write the letters.**

___ ___ ___ ___ ___
2   14

Review Units 1 and 2

1 Look and write the word.

9
T

8

7 **1** O

2 L

3

4

5

6

2 Read and circle the answer.

1 What are … ? They're books.
   a this   **b** (these)

2 He … a motorcycle.
   a has   **b** does

3 … babies.
   a It's   **b** They're

4 How do you … "Leo"? L-E-O.
   a spell   **b** name

5 … she … a boat?
   a Does, have   **b** Have, does

6 Is … beautiful? Yes, … is.
   a it, it   **b** they, they

3 Look, read, and match.

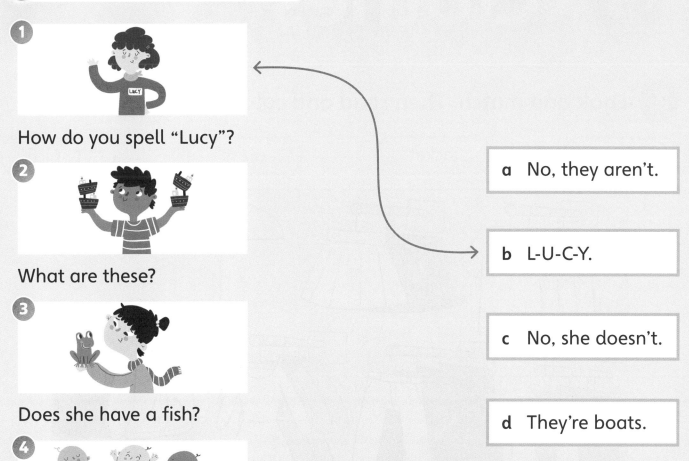

1 How do you spell "Lucy"?

2 What are these?

3 Does she have a fish?

4 Are they old?

a No, they aren't.

b L-U-C-Y.

c No, she doesn't.

d They're boats.

4 🎧 2.17 Listen and check ✓.

1

2

3 Clothes

1 **Look and match. Then read and color.**

shoes   jacket   dress   T-shirt

skirt   socks   jeans   shirt   pants

1 Color the shoes black.
2 Color the pants green.
3 Color the jacket yellow.
4 Color the T-shirt purple.
5 Color the jeans blue.
6 Color the skirt orange.
7 Color the shirt red.
8 Color the socks blue.
9 Color the dress pink.

2   **Listen and stick.**

1

2

3

4

5

3 Think **Look and write the words.**

~~socks~~   jeans   T-shirt   skirt
pants   shirt   shoes   jacket

1 _____

2 _____ →

3 _____

4 _____

5 _____ →

6 _____

7 socks →

8 _____

My picture dictionary → Go to page 87: Check the words you know and trace.

4 Look, read, and check ✓.

1

What are you wearing? I'm wearing pants and a shirt.

2

What are you wearing? I'm wearing a dress and shoes.

3

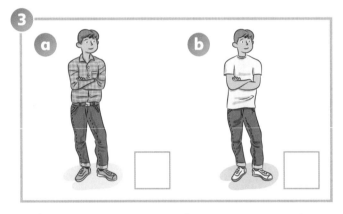

What are you wearing? I'm wearing jeans and a T-shirt.

4

What are you wearing? I'm wearing a skirt and a shirt.

5 Look at the pictures and write.

1  **2**  **3**  **4**

1 I'm wearing _a skirt_ , _a T-shirt_ , and _shoes_ .

2 I'm wearing _____ , _____ , and _____ .

3 I'm wearing _____ , _____ , and _____ .

4 I'm wearing _____ , _____ , and _____ .

6  **Listen and number the pictures.**

 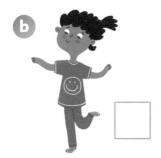 

7 **Look, read, and circle the word.**

Are you wearing a (skirt) / **dress**?

No, I'm not.

Are you wearing **shoes** / **socks**?

No, I'm not.

Are you wearing a **shirt** / **T-shirt**?

Yes, I am.

Are you wearing **pants** / **jeans**?

Yes, I am.

8 (About Me) **Draw. Ask and answer with a friend.**

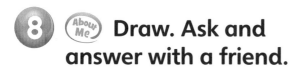

Are you wearing a skirt?

No, I'm not.

a Here you are, iPal. You can use my hat.

Thank you.

And my jacket.

b Look at these clothes!

Here's a hat for you! **1**

c Look at me!

Fantastic!

d What are you wearing?

They're clothes for a party!

e First prize ... The robot!

Thanks. But I'm not a robot!

f A party?

Yes, look! I'm wearing big pants and long shoes.

10 Look, read, and stick.

I share things.

11 Trace the letters.

 Jackals don't like jello. Yaks don't like yogurt.

12 Listen and circle *j* or *y*.

1  **2**  **3**  **4**

j y   j y   j y   j y

What are clothes made of?

1 **Look and write the number.**

wool ☐   silk ☐   leather ☐   cotton 1

2 **Look, read, and circle the word.**

wool / (silk)   leather / cotton   wool / silk   cotton / leather

Evaluation

1 **Write the words and find.**

1 socks

2 _____

3 _____

4 _____

5 _____

```
g s k i r t f s h o e s d
f s d r e s s d v b c m q
j e a n s n a j k o a l o
a w t q o p a n t s p l l
s o c k s m c n v b w i k
```

6 _____

2 **What's your favorite part? Use your stickers.**

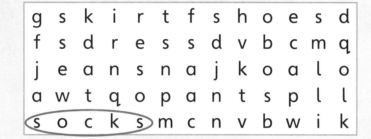

story   song   video

3 Puzzle **What's different? Circle and write.**
Then go to page 93 and write the letters.

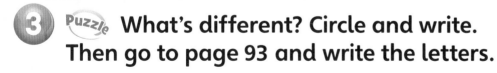

____ ____ ____ ____
    11   12

4 Rooms

1 Look, read, and circle the word.

closet / (bookcase)

lamp / mirror

TV / phone

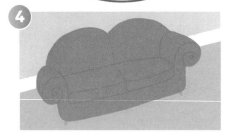

couch / cabinet

clock / TV

bookcase / table

2 Look, read, and write.

It isn't a cabinet. It isn't a bookcase. It's a ___closet___ .

It isn't a mirror. It isn't a lamp. It's a _____ .

It isn't a table. It isn't a bed. It's a _____ .

It isn't a TV. It isn't a lamp. It's a _____ .

3 🎧 4.05 ✂️ **Listen and stick.**

1	2	3

4	5

4 (Think) **Look, match, and write the words.**

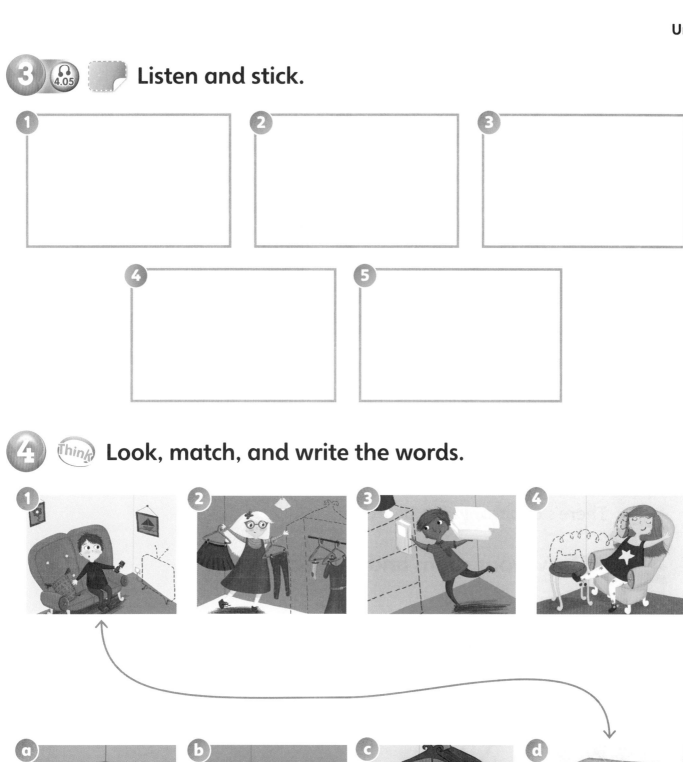

_____   _____   _____   TV _____

My picture dictionary ⟶ Go to page 88: Check the words you know and trace.

5 Look, read, and write *yes* or *no*.

1 There are four lamps in the bedroom.   _no_

2 There are two couches in the living room.   _____

3 There are two clocks in the bedroom.   _____

4 There's a closet in the living room.   _____

5 There's a bookcase in the living room.   _____

6 There's a mirror in the bedroom.   _____

6 (About Me) Draw your room and say. Then write.

There's a lamp in my room.

There are two tables in my room.

There's a _____ in my room.

There are _____

_____ in my room.

7 **What's next? Read and write.**

| fifteen | twenty | ~~eleven~~ | twelve |

1 one, three, five, seven, nine, ___eleven___
2 two, four, six, eight, ten, _____ , fourteen
3 three, six, nine, twelve, _____ , eighteen
4 five, ten, fifteen, _____

8 **Count and write. Then answer the questions.**

12					

1 How many socks are there?   _There are twelve socks._
2 How many fish are there?   _____
3 How many cars are there?   _____
4 How many shoes are there?   _____
5 How many balls are there?   _____
6 How many books are there?   _____

9 🎧 4.11 Read and write the letter. Then listen and check.

a Let's clean up. **b** Thanks, iPal! **c** It's your ring, Tina!

d Look at this big bookcase! **e** Oh, no! Where's my ring?

f Now it's neat.

1

e

Is it in the art set?

2

There's my doll. We're in my bedroom!

3

Let's go in. Walk on me!

4

What a mess!

5

Let's put the toys in the cabinet.

6

What does iPal have?

10 **Look, read, and stick.**

I'm neat.

11 **Trace the letters.**

Meerkats have mouths. Newts have noses.

12  **Listen and circle the pictures.**

m

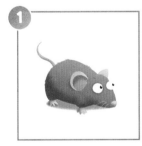

n

How many are there?

1 Count and write the number.

1
 +  =

2
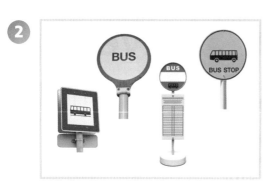 +  =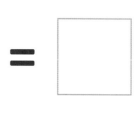

3
 +  =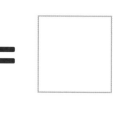

4
 +  =

Evaluation

1 Order the letters and write the word.

1 mlpa _lamp_

2 abetl _____

3 ccklo _____

4 hepno _____

5 mrrroi _____

6 houcc _____

2 What's your favorite part? Use your stickers.

story   song   video

3 **Puzzle** What's different? Circle and write.
Then go to page 93 and write the letters.

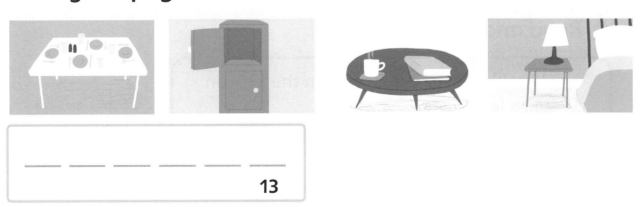

‗ ‗ ‗ ‗ ‗ ‗
13

Review Units 3 and 4

1 Look and write the word. Then draw Number 8.

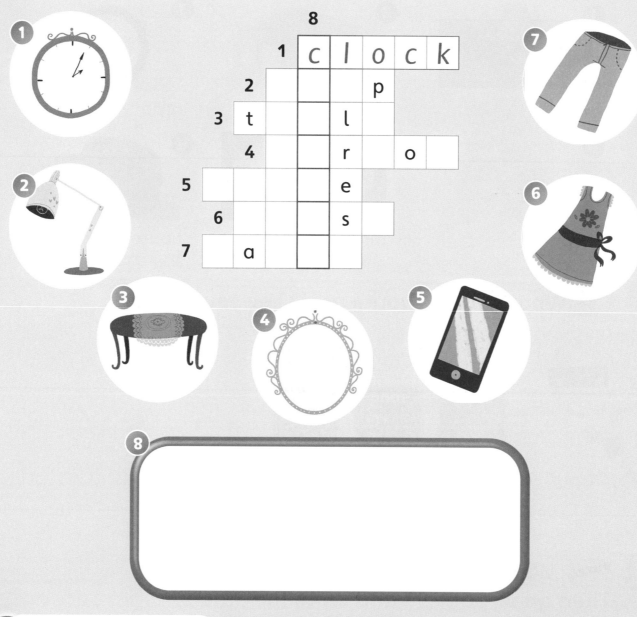

```
              8
        1  c  l  o  c  k
     2            p
  3  t           l
     4           r     o
  5              e
  6              s
  7     a
```

8

2 Read and circle.

1 **There's** / **There are** a table in the kitchen.
2 What **is** / **are** you wearing?
3 How many bookcases **are** / **is** there?
4 This is a yellow **dress** / **jeans**.

3 Look, read, and write the answers.

1

Is it ugly? _No, it isn't._

2

Are you wearing a jacket, Simon?

_____

3

What are you wearing, Grandma?

_____

4

How many socks are there in the closet? _____

4 🎧 4.17 Listen and check ✓.

1

2

5 Meals

1 Find and circle. Look and write the word.

1

rice

2

_____

3

_____

4

_____

5

_____

6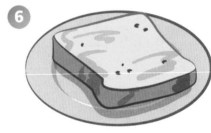

_____

peascarrotscereal(rice)toastfish

2 Look, read, and write *yes* or *no*.

1 There's meat on the table.
_____ _yes_ _____

2 There are peas on the table.
_____

3 There are potatoes on the table. _____

4 There are sausages on the table. _____

5 There's cereal on the table.
_____

3 🎧 5.05 📄 **Listen and stick.**

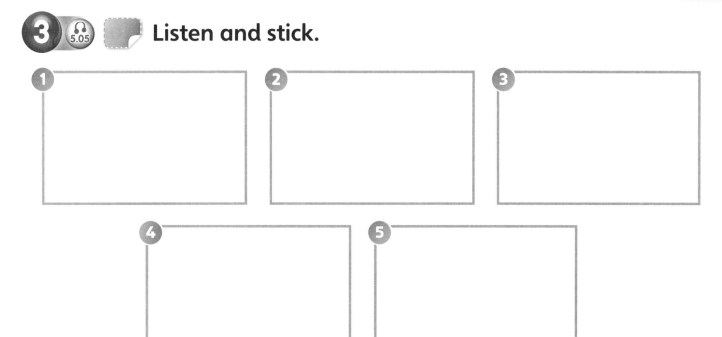

1	2	3

4	5

4 Think **Look and write the words.**

| toast   cereal   peas   rice   meat |
| fish   sausages   potatoes   carrots |

These foods are plants.	These foods aren't plants.
toast	

My picture dictionary Go to page 89: Check the words you know and trace.

Vocabulary **49**

5 5.08 **Listen and match. Draw a happy face or a sad face.**

6 **Look, read, and circle the words.**

She **(likes)** / **doesn't like** fish.

He **likes** / **doesn't like** cereal.

She **likes** / **doesn't like** meat.

He **likes** / **doesn't like** peas.

7 **Look, read, and circle the words. Then answer the questions.**

Kim

Jim

1 Does Kim like (cereal) / **sausages**?
Yes, she does.

2 Does Kim like **toast** / **peas**?
No, she doesn't.

3 Does Kim like toast, for breakfast?
Yes, she does.

4 Does Kim like sausages?
_____

1 Does Jim like **carrots** / **potatoes**?
Yes, he does.

2 Does Jim like **steak** / **fish**?
No, he doesn't.

3 Does Jim like steak, for lunch?
_____

4 Does Jim like potatoes?
_____

8   **Draw and say. Then write and circle.**

My mom likes meat and carrots for dinner. She doesn't like fish.

My _____ likes _____ and _____ for dinner. He / She doesn't like _____ .

likes   fish   please   ~~lunch~~   peas   Cake

1

Look! Café Hawaii!

Let's go for _lunch_ !

2

Would you like _____ and potatoes?

Yes, please!   No, thank you!

3

What about carrots or _____ , iPal?

No, thank you!

4

Oh, dear! What would you like, iPal?

_____ ! I like chocolate cake.

5

More cake, _____ !

No, iPal. That's enough!

6

What's the matter?

He _____ chocolate cake – a lot!

10 **Look, read, and stick.**

I eat healthy food.

11 **Trace the letters.**

A seal in the sun. A zebra in the zoo.

12 (5.14) **Listen and circle s or z.**

1

S Z

2

S Z

3

S Z

4

S Z

What kind of **food** is it?

1 Look and write the words in the chart.

peas

sausages

rice

carrots

fish

cheese

milk

bread

fruits and vegetables	meat and fish	grains and cereals	dairy
peas			

Evaluation

1 **Read and write the word.**

1 T _o_ _a_ _s_ _t_ is bread.
2 C _ _ _ _ _ _ _ are orange. They come from plants.
3 F _ _ _ live in water. They can swim.
4 P _ _ _ are very small and green. They come from plants.
5 Chicken and sausages are m _ _ _ _ .
6 R _ _ _ is small and white. It comes from plants.

2 **What's your favorite part? Use your stickers.**

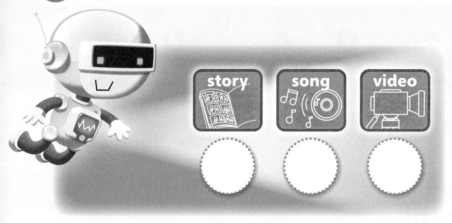

story   song   video

3 **Puzzle** **What's different? Circle and write.**
Then go to page 93 and write the letters.

___ ___ ___ ___
4   16

6 Activities

1 (Think) **Look, match, and write.**

1 2 3 4

a ride a _____

b play _____

c fly a _____

d take *photographs*

2 **Look and write the words.**

~~play~~   take   ride   fly   play   roller-skate

1 A: Let's play tennis. Can you __play__ tennis?

B: No, I can't, but I can _____ basketball.

2 A: Can you _____ a horse?

B: Yes, I can, and I can _____ a kite, too.

3 A: I can roller-skate. Can you _____ ?

B: No, I can't, but I can _____ photographs!

3 Listen and stick.

4 Think **Look and write the words.**

ride a horse ~~play basketball~~ play tennis
roller-skate take photographs play baseball

play basketball

My picture dictionary → Go to page 90: Check the words you know and trace.

Vocabulary **57**

5 **Look at the chart. Circle the words and write.**

	May	Tom	Jill	Sam
✓ like	fly a kite	play basketball	play baseball	roller-skate
✗ don't like	play tennis	play field hockey	ride a horse	take photographs

1  I **like /** ⟨**don't like**⟩ playing tennis.

2  I **like / don't like** playing field hockey.

3  I **like / don't like** riding a horse.

4  I **like / don't like** taking photographs.

5 May ___*likes*___ flying a kite.

6 Tom _____ playing basketball.

7 Jill _____ playing baseball.

8 Sam _____ roller-skating.

6 **Look, read, and circle the answers.**

1

Do you like taking photographs?

Yes, I do. / No, I don't.

2

Do you like playing tennis?

Yes, I do. / No, I don't.

3

Does he like playing baseball?

Yes, he does. / No, he doesn't.

4

Does she like flying a kite?

Yes, she does. / No, she doesn't.

7 (About Me) **Complete the chart. Ask and answer.**

Do you like riding a horse?

Yes, I do.

No, I don't.

Do you like …	riding a horse?	_____ ?	_____ ?
1 Me	yes / no	yes / no	yes / no
2 _____	yes / no	yes / no	yes / no
3 _____	yes / no	yes / no	yes / no

I like …

_____ likes …

8 🎧 6.11 Read and number. Then listen and check.

a

Good job, Olivia!

Thanks, iPal.

b

I'm sorry.

That's OK.

c

The *All Stars* are my favorite team!

Let's play! Put on these shirts!

d

Watch me! Throw the ball like this.

Yes!

e

That's not fair!

Play nicely, iPal.

f

It's a basketball!

Are you OK, David?

1

9 **Look, unscramble, and stick.**

I (lypa) _____ nicely.

10 **Trace the letters.**

A camel with a camera. A kangaroo with a kite.

11 **Listen and number the pictures.**

a

b

c

d

e  1

f

What equipment do we need?

1 **Look and match the pictures.**

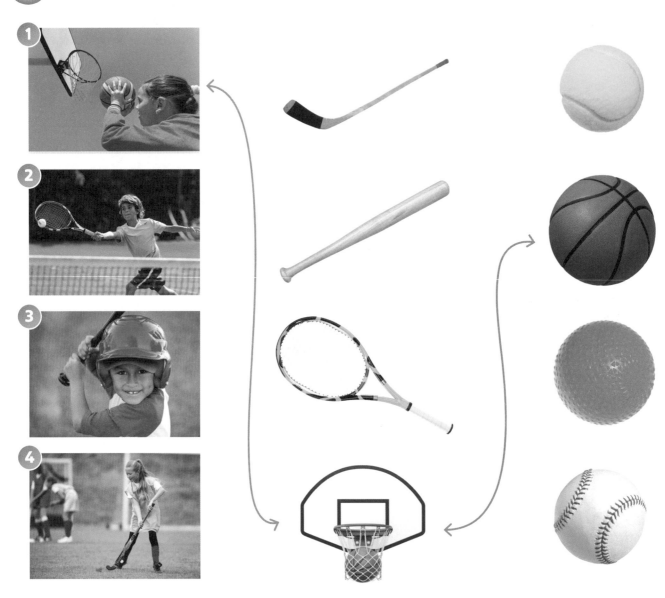

2 **Look at Activity 1 and write the words.**

1 I play basketball with a ___basket___ and a ___ball___ .
2 I play tennis with a _____ and a _____ .
3 I play baseball with a _____ and a _____ .
4 I play field hockey with a _____ and a _____ .

Evaluation

1 **Look and write the activity.**

1 r_oller-skate_

2 p_____ b_____

3 r_____ a h_____

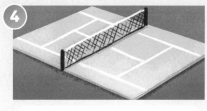
4 p_____ t_____

5 p_____ f_____
h_____

6 p_____ b_____

2 **What's your favorite part? Use your stickers.**

 story
 song
 video

3 **Puzzle** **What's different? Circle and write.**
Then go to page 93 and write the letters.

_____ _____ _____   _____   _____ _____ _____ _____ _____
15   6   5

Review Units 5 and 6

1 Write and draw.

a	b	c	d	e	f	g	h	i	k	l	o	p	r	s	t	u	y
1	2	3	4	5	6	7	8	9	10	11	12	13	14	15	16	17	18

1

_p o t a t o e s_
13 12 16 1 16 12 5 15

2

_ _ _ _ _ _ _ _
6 11 18 1 10 9 16 5

3

_ _ _ _ _ _ _ _
15 1 17 15 1 7 5 15

4

_ _ _ _ _ _ _ _ _ _ _ _
13 11 1 18 2 1 15 10 5 16 2 1 11 11

5

_ _ _ _ _ _
3 5 14 5 1 11

6

_ _ _ _ _ _ - _ _ _ _
14 12 11 11 5 14 15 10 1 16 5

2 Read and match.

1 He likes
2 She doesn't
3 Does he
4 I like playing
5 He doesn't like
6 Do you like

a field hockey.
b beans.
c taking photographs?
d toast.
e like playing tennis?
f like meat.

3 Look, read, and write the words.

roller-skating   rice   ~~photographs~~   fish   ~~do~~   doesn't   does   don't

1

Do you like taking _photographs_ ?
Yes, I _do_ .

2

Does she like _____ ?
Yes, she _____ .

3

Does he like _____ ?
No, he _____ .

4

Do you like _____ ?
No, I _____ .

4 🎧 6.17 Listen and check ✔.

1

2

65

In town

1 **Look at the picture and write the letter.**

1 street __e__   **2** café _____
3 school _____   **4** bookstore _____
5 playground _____   **6** supermarket _____

2 **Look at Activity 1 and write _yes_ or _no_.**

1 There's a toy store in the town.   __no__
2 There's a playground in the town.   _____
3 There's a movie theater in the town.   _____
4 There's a café in the town.   _____
5 There's a clothing store in the town.   _____
6 There's a school in the town.   _____

3 **Listen and stick.**

1.

2.

3.

4.

5.

4 Think **Look and write.**

1.

toy store

2.

3.

4.

My picture dictionary → Go to page 91: Check the words you know and trace.

5 (Think) **Look, read, and match.**

1 next to

2 in front of

3 behind

4 between

6 **Look, read, and circle the words.**

1 The school is **behind** / **next to** the playground.

2 The toy store is **in front of** / **between** the bookstore and the clothing store.

3 The tree is **next to** / **in front of** the movie theater.

4 The supermarket is **behind** / **between** the park.

7 (About Me) **Draw and say. Then write.**

My school is next to the park.

My school is _____
_____ .

8 Look, read, and check ✓.

1 Is there a toy store next to the school?

Yes, there is. ☐ No, there isn't. ✓

2 Is there a café in front of the supermarket?

Yes, there is. ☐ No, there isn't. ☐

3 Is there a toy store between the bookstore and the school?

Yes, there is. ☐ No, there isn't. ☐

4 Is there a playground behind the school?

Yes, there is. ☐ No, there isn't. ☐

9 Complete the questions and the answers.

1 _____Is there_____ a park next to the bookstore?
No, _____there isn't_____ .

2 _____ a playground between the school and the supermarket?
No, _____ .

3 _____ a street in front of the café?
Yes, _____ .

4 _____ a park behind the supermarket?
Yes, _____ .

10 🎧 7.11 Read and write the letter. Then listen and check.

a No, iPal! Be careful!

b I like going to the movies.

c Movie tickets!

d Oh, no! It's closed today!

e Look left and right.

f Where's the movie theater?

11 Look, unscramble, and stick.

I am (esfa) _____ .

12 Trace the letters.

A quick queen bee. An ox with an X-ray.

13 (7.14) Listen and write *qu* or *x*.

①

_qu_een bee

② **6**

si__

③

o__

④

__ick

Where are the places?

1 Look, read, and circle the word.

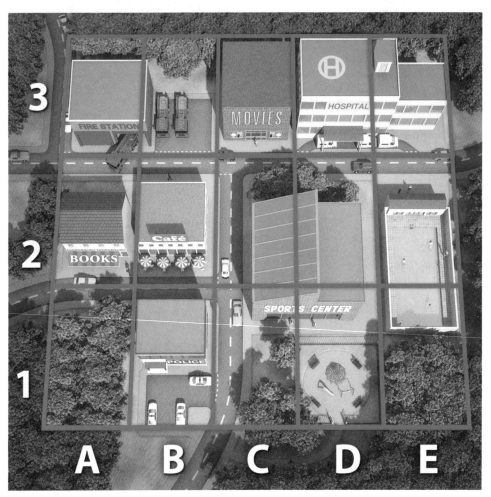

1 There's a (fire station)/ **police station** in A3.
2 There's a **movie theater** / **bookstore** in C3.
3 There's a **café** / **hospital** in B2.
4 There's a **sports center** / **park** in D1.

2 Look at Activity 1 and answer the questions.

1 Where's the police station?   _B1_
2 Where's the bookstore?   _____
3 Where's the hospital?   _____
4 Where's the sports center?   _____

Evaluation

1  **Look and write the word.**

1

supermarket

2

_____

3

_____

4

_____

5

_____

6

_____

2 **What's your favorite part? Use your stickers.**

story   song   video

3 **Puzzle What's different? Circle and write.**
Then go to page 93 and write the letters.

TOYS   TOYS   TOYS

___ ___ ___ ___ ___ ___ ___ ___
    3   9

8 On the farm

1 Look, read, and circle the word.

1 **cow** / horse

2 sheep / goat

3 barn / field

4 horse / donkey

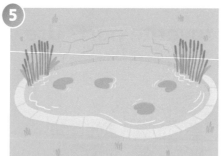
5 field / pond

6 duck / donkey

2 Follow the animal words.

Start →

cow	goat	park	barn
field	duck	sheep	air
hospital	grains	donkey	school
dairy	pond	cat	horse

Good job!

3 8.05 **Listen and stick.**

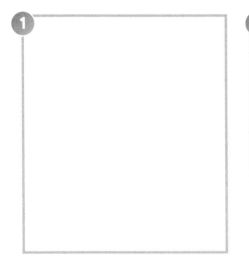

4 Think **Read and write the word.**

1 Milk comes from this animal. It isn't a goat. ____cow____

2 This animal can swim and fly. It likes water. _____

3 We can ride this animal. It's not a donkey. _____

4 Wool comes from this animal. _____

5 This is a house for cows and horses. _____

6 Fish and ducks swim in this. _____

My picture dictionary → Go to page 92: Check the words you know and trace.

5 Look, read, and check ✓.

1

The cow is eating. ✓

The cow is jumping. ☐

2

The horse is running. ☐

The horse is sleeping. ☐

3

The duck is flying. ☐

The duck is swimming. ☐

6 Look, read, and answer the questions.

1

What's the donkey doing?

It's eating.

2

What's the duck doing?

_____

3

What's the goat doing?

_____

4

What's the sheep doing?

_____

7 (About Me) Draw your favorite farm animal. Then write.

This is a _____ .

It's _____ .

8 8.09 Listen and check ✓ or put an ✗.

1

 ✓

2

 ☐

3

 ☐

4

☐

9 Look, read, and circle the word.

1

Is the horse **eating** / (**sleeping**)?
No, it isn't.

2

Is the cow **running** / **sleeping**?
Yes, it is.

3

Is the goat **sleeping** / **jumping**?
No, it isn't.

4

Is the duck **swimming** / **flying**?
Yes, it is.

5

Is the sheep **eating** / **running**?
No, it isn't.

6

Is the horse **sleeping** / **swimming**?
No, it isn't.

(8.11) **Look and write the words. Then listen and check.**

party   iPal   dancing   Goodbye   flying   Welcome

1

It's a message for __iPal__.

Let's find him!

2

Would you like to come to a _____?

Yes, please!

3

Hold on!

We're _____!

4

_____ to the party!

It's so nice to see you!

WELCOME HOME iPAL

5

What's Ben doing?

He's ... _____!

6

_____, iPal!

Goodbye! Thanks for taking care of me!

Look, unscramble, and stick.

I love my (ehmo) _____ .

12 Trace the letters.

A wolf in the water.
A white whale with
a wheel.

13 🎧 8.14 **Listen and put a check ✓ next to *w* or *wh*.**

1	w ✓	wh ☐	2	w ☐	wh ☐
3	w ☐	wh ☐	4	w ☐	wh ☐

What do **farmers** do?

1 Look and number the pictures.

a

b

c

d

1

2 Look at Activity 1 and write the letter.

1 A farmer turns soil. | b |

2 A farmer plants seeds. | |

3 A farmer waters plants. | |

4 A farmer harvests plants. | |

Evaluation

1 **Write the words and find.**

1. _COW_
2. _____
3. _____
4. _____
5. _____
6. _____

```
s h e e p a c n (c o w) o
g a d o n k e y m k l p
c b a r n o l p a t u e
f i e l d g h n a o q i
a f p o n d g r t e y a
```

2 **What's your favorite part? Use your stickers.**

story   song   video

3 **Puzzle** **What's different? Circle and write.**
Then go to page 93 and write the letters.

____ ____ ____ ____
7   18

Review Units 7 and 8

1 Look and write the word. Then draw Number 11.

1 | s u p e r m a r k e t

2 Look, read, and write the answers.

1

What's the goat doing?

It's jumping.

2

Is there a park next to the supermarket?

_____

3

Is the sheep running?

_____

4

What's the horse doing?

_____

3  Listen and check ✓.

1

2

Hello again!

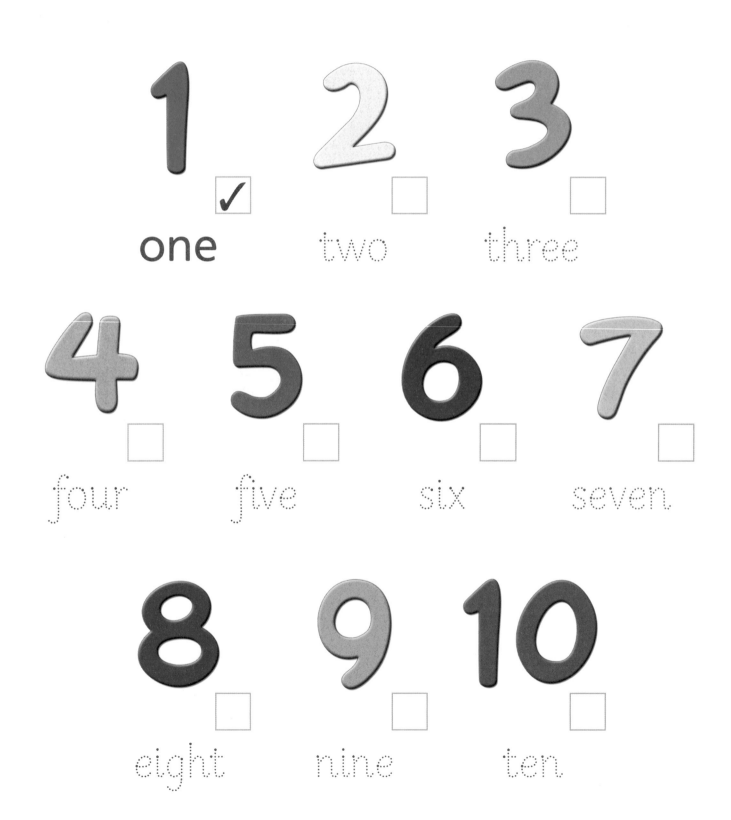

1 ✓ one

2 ☐ two

3 ☐ three

4 ☐ four

5 ☐ five

6 ☐ six

7 ☐ seven

8 ☐ eight

9 ☐ nine

10 ☐ ten

bus ✓

boat ☐

car ☐

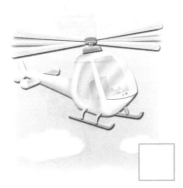

helicopter ☐

truck ☐

motorcycle ☐

plane ☐

tractor ☐

train ☐

baby ✓

boy

cat

dog

fish

frog

girl

man

mouse

woman

3 Clothes

 ✓
dress

 ☐
jacket

 ☐
jeans

 ☐
shirt

 ☐
shoes

 ☐
skirt

 ☐
socks

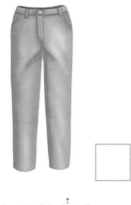 ☐
pants

 ☐
T-shirt

(4) Rooms

 ✓
bookcase

clock

cabinet

lamp

mirror

phone

couch

table

TV

closet

beans ✓

carrots ☐

cereal ☐

fish ☐

meat ☐

peas ☐

potatoes ☐

rice ☐

sausages ☐

toast ☐

fly a kite ✔

play baseball ☐

play basketball ☐

play field hockey ☐

take photographs ☐

ride a horse ☐

roller-skate ☐

play tennis ☐

(7) In town

 ✓
bookstore

café

movie
theater

clothing
store

park

play-
ground

school

street

supermarket

toy store

8 On the farm

barn ✓

cow

donkey

duck

field

goat

horse

pond

sheep

My puzzle

1 Write the letters in the correct place.

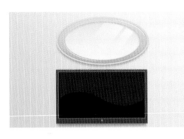